ULTIMATE SPORTS

FREEZE YOUR FEAR!

EXTREME SNOW AND ICE SPORTS

CHERITON
CHILDREN'S BOOKS

Published in 2024 by **Cheriton Children's Books**
1 Bank Drive West, Shrewsbury, Shropshire, SY3 9DJ, UK

© 2024 Cheriton Children's Books

First Edition

Author: Sarah Eason
Designer: Paul Myerscough
Editor: Jennifer Sanderson
Proofreader: Katie Dicker

Printed in China

Please visit our website,
www.cheritonchildrensbooks.com
to see more of our high-quality books.

CONTENTS

FREEZE YOUR FEAR!

With the changing seasons, parts of our amazing planet become covered with snow and ice. Other places are a permanent winter wonderland. But for some of Earth's **elite** sportspeople, all are go-to adventure playgrounds. For them, these wintery wonderworlds were made for sport—and they have taken these sports to the extreme.

READY TO EXPLORE THE EXTREME?...

THE EXTREME DREAM

For centuries, people have come up with supersmart ways to get across snow and ice. They have climbed freezing mountains, clinging to their icy peaks. They have used **sleds** to travel across wintery landscapes, **venturing** into the wilderness. And they have used skis to travel across snow-covered lands. But what was once necessary has today become fun and for some, the ultimate sport.

...THEN, FREEZE YOUR FEAR AND GET SET TO TAKE ON THE COLD!

CHAPTER 1

SKI, BOARD, AND KITE IT!

In the winter wonderland that is the world of snow, sport really comes to life. From skiing and snowboarding to snow kiting, head to the slopes and you'll see extreme sports at their best.

OLD SPORT, NEW EXTREME!

Check out the world's snowy slopes and you'll find skiers of all ages racing across them. But there is nothing new about skiing—it has a long history, dating back more than 5,000 years. However, over time, people have become more and more adventurous with their skiing, and today it has become one of the planet's most exciting and popular extreme sports.

Cross-country skiing is an amazing way to see the landscape.

"THE BEST SKIER ON THE MOUNTAIN IS THE ONE HAVING THE MOST FUN."

Freestyle skiing showcases incredible moves.

STUNTS, TRICKS, AND TOURS

There are many different styles of skiing, including alpine, cross-country, freestyle, and ski touring. Alpine skiing, also known as downhill skiing, involves skiing down slopes and **trails** at ski resorts. In cross-country skiing, skiers travel over flatter **terrain**. This type of skiing is often done for fitness or as a way to explore the outdoors. In freestyle, skiers perform amazing tricks and jumps, often in **terrain parks** or on **halfpipes**. Ski touring is traveling on skis over **backcountry** terrain, often with special equipment, such as climbing aids, which helps skiers get up steep slopes.

SKI FOR FUN, SKI FOR SPORT

Over time, people began to ski for fun. In the late nineteenth century, skiing became very popular in the Alpine region of Europe. Skiing then made its way to North America in the early twentieth century, and it quickly spread to other parts of the world. The sport has also been a competitive sport for many years, and is included in the Winter Olympic Games.

SKI STEP UP

For some skiers, ordinary skiing is not enough—they have taken their skis to the slopes and the sport to the extreme. Also known as freeride skiing, extreme skiing involves taking on challenging and dangerous terrain, such as steep slopes, narrow **chutes**, and rugged backcountry routes.

GOING OFF-PISTE

Freeride skiers go **off-piste** in unmarked terrain, in mountainous places. They challenge themselves with jumps off cliffs and other obstacles. Extreme skiers often seek out new and unexplored terrain, pushing the limits of what is possible.

HEADING UP HIGH

As well as skiing off-piste, the sport also involves big mountain skiing, ski mountaineering, and heli-skiing. Big mountain skiing is skiing in steep and rugged mountain terrain, while ski mountaineering combines skiing and mountaineering to climb and ski steep peaks and **glaciers**. In heli-skiing, skiers travel by helicopter to difficult-to-reach ski terrain.

EXTREME STAR

ADVENTURE SEEKER

Cody Townsend is an American **professional** skier and filmmaker known for his adventurous approach to skiing. Cody was born on March 14, 1983, in Santa Cruz, California, and grew up skiing in the nearby Sierra Nevada Mountains.

Extreme skiing requires a high level of technical skill.

Freeride skiers need to be prepared and very experienced. The sport requires great mental and physical fitness.

BABY SKIER

Cody was named after Cody Peak in Jackson Hole, Wyoming, and was skiing by the time he was just two years old. He fell in love with the sport, and decided by age six that his goal in life was to be a professional skier- and then, Cody did just that.

FREESTYLE AND FAME

Cody began his skiing career in the early 2000s, first competing in freestyle and big mountain events. He then stepped up to backcountry skiing and ski mountaineering. In 2014, Cody became famous for skiing "The Crack," an extremely narrow and steep chute in the Tordrillo Mountains of Southwest Alaska.

FILMMAKER AND THE FIFTY

As well as his career as a skier, Cody is also a filmmaker. He has produced and **directed** several skiing **documentaries**, including "Days of My Youth" and "The Fifty," in which he attempted to ski the 50 toughest downhill runs in North America. When he isn't filming, Cody is on film! He performs **stunts** for movies and is considered one of the most adventurous skiers on the planet.

"THE MOUNTAIN IS THE BOSS, AND YOU'D BETTER CHECK YOUR EGO AT THE DOOR."

KITE MEETS SNOW

What happens when you take a kite, add some skis or a board, and snow? Snow kiting! In this extreme winter sport, a skier or snowboarder travels over snow-covered terrain pulled along by a kite. The rider uses the kite to capture the wind, creating power to **propel** themselves across the snow.

RIDE AND RACE

There are several different styles of snow kiting, including freeride, freestyle, and racing. Freeride snow kiting involves exploring open terrain and mountains. Freestyle snow kiting showcases tricks and jumps, often in terrain parks. In snow kite racing, riders compete on a racecourse, typically on flat, open terrain.

EXTREME HISTORY

Snow kiting began in the early 2000s as a variation of kitesurfing—a similar sport that is done on water. Snow kiting has since become incredibly popular, particularly in areas with reliable wind and large areas of snow-covered terrain. Top snow kiting places are Scandinavia, Canada, and the Rocky Mountains in the United States.

Snow kiting can be done on flat, open terrain or in mountainous regions.

Snow kiting requires a combination of skiing or snowboarding skills, kite-flying skills, and an understanding of wind patterns.

TRICKS AND STUNTS

Some extreme snow kiting includes performing tricks, jumps, and **maneuvers** in challenging and often dangerous terrain, such as steep mountain slopes and backcountry areas. It requires a high level of technical skill, physical fitness, and mental focus. Snow kiters must have a great understanding of wind patterns and **avalanche** safety.

KNOW THE DANGERS

While extreme snow kiting is very exciting, it can also be dangerous. This is especially true in backcountry terrain, where avalanches pose a serious danger. Snow kiters must be experienced and well prepared, with proper training, equipment, and safety gear.

"SNOW KITING IS LIKE DANCING WITH NATURE."

Today, snowboarding has also become a way of life for many boarders, creating a whole new style of fashion, music, and art.

BOARD MEETS SNOW

One of the most extraordinary snow sports to watch has to be snowboarding. In this extreme winter sport, people ride a board over snow-covered terrain, such as mountains, hills, or **snow parks**.

BUILT LIKE A SKATEBOARD, BUT FOR SNOW

The board used for snowboarding is similar in shape to a skateboard, but larger and wider. The rider stands with both feet strapped onto the board, and moves their body to control the board and **navigate** the slope.

FREER, BIGGER, AND BETTER

Over the years, snowboarding has changed and grown, with different styles being added to the sport. They include freestyle, big air, halfpipe, backcountry, and more.

TAKING IT TO AN EXTREME

Extreme snowboarding, also known as freeriding, is a form of snowboarding that involves riding off-piste. Boarders head off in search of natural terrain features such as cliffs, chutes, trees, and fresh **powder**. The goal of extreme snowboarding is to ride down steep, challenging terrain while performing amazing tricks and maneuvers.

"THERE'S NO FEELING LIKE SNOWBOARDING!"

More and more people are taking to extreme snowboarding.

A RISK WORTH TAKING

Extreme snowboarding is a high-risk activity with a lot of potential dangers, including avalanches, **tree wells**, and collisions with rocks and other obstacles. Boarders need to be incredibly fit, have great technical ability, and be very safety aware.

PUSH TO THE LIMITS

Why do people extreme snowboard when it is so dangerous? For many, it's the thrill of pushing themselves to the limit and experiencing the rush of **adrenaline** that comes with the sport.

BODY AND SOUL

Another reason people do extreme snowboarding is to explore the outdoors and experience the beauty of snowy mountains and landscapes. Snowboarding can take people to **remote** and unspoiled places that are difficult to reach in any other way. Extreme snowboarding can also be a chance to escape the stresses of daily life and experience a sense of freedom and adventure.

EXTREME NEED TO KNOW

Due to the risks of the sport, many extreme snowboarders carry specialized equipment, such as **avalanche beacons**, shovels, and **probes**. They often ride in groups with experienced guides or partners.

Extreme snowboarding requires a high level of skill, concentration, and physical ability.

Many boarders find snowboarding helps them clear their mind and connect with nature.

EXTREME STAR

TEENAGE STAR

Born in 2000, one of the most successful riders in recent years is Chloe Kim. This young American snowboarder burst onto the scene as a teenager and has since become a household name.

ONE OF THE GREATS

Despite her young age, Chloe is already considered one of the greatest female snowboarders of all time, and is sure to continue making snowboarding headlines for years to come.

OLYMPIC HONORS

Chloe is known for her great skill, amazing jumps, and stylish riding. She won gold in the women's halfpipe at the 2018 Olympics in Pyeongchang, South Korea, making her the youngest woman in history to win the event. She has also won many X Games gold medals and FIS World Championship medals.

CHLOE DESCRIBES SNOWBOARDING AS AN ART FORM—EVERY SNOWBOARDER HAS THEIR OWN STYLE.

Chloe is also passionate about causes such as **climate change** and **gender equality**, and regularly speaks out about them.

THE WORLD'S BEST BOARDING

For elite snowboarders, Earth's snowy heights have a wealth of challenges. But of them all, these are considered some of the best places to board.

Alyeska Resort

Where: Alaska

The draw: the largest resort in Alaska, it provides some of the most amazing snowboarding experiences in the world

Chamonix

Where: France

The draw: snowboarding heaven for extreme snowboarding, with its steep, **glaciated** terrain that provides great off-piste riding

La Grave

Where: France

The draw: challenging off-piste routes—expert snowboarding skills and knowledge are needed here!

Niseko

Where: Japan

The draw: a lot of snowfall, mixed terrain, and beautiful hot springs

Whistler

Where: Canada

The draw: its backcountry is famous for steep, powder-filled chutes and **bowls**

CHAPTER 2

SKATE IT, SLED IT!

Skis and snowboards are not the only way to experience extreme snow and ice sports. Sleighs and skates take people on breathtakingly fast and exciting trips across snow and ice.

DOWNHILL—FAST!

Bobsleighing also known as bobsledding, is about as extreme as you can get. In this fast and furious winter sport, teams of two or four **athletes** make timed runs down a narrow, twisting ice track in a **gravity**-powered sled. Athletes push the sled at the start of the run, and then jump inside it. They navigate the course using their body weight to steer and control the sled.

DANGEROUS AND DEMANDING

Bobsleighing is a dangerous sport, with the potential for crashes and serious injuries. For that reason, safety equipment such as helmets and protective padding must be worn. Athletes must also go through extreme training and preparation to compete at the highest level.

Bobsledders run with the sled to pick up speed, then jump on board.

"BOBSLEDDING IS LIKE BEING PART OF A TEAM OF SUPERHEROES!"

Bobsleighing first took place in Switzerland in the late nineteenth century. It earned its name after competitors used the technique of bobbing back and forth to increase the speed of the sled. The first organized race was held in St. Moritz, Switzerland, in 1898. The sport grew quickly, spreading across Europe and making its way to North America.

Skeleton began in Switzerland too, also in the late nineteenth century. Although a men's race featured in the 1948 Olympics, it was thought to be dangerous, and so was stopped until 2002, when it was reintroduced for men and women at the Games.

THE SKELETON

Extreme bobsleighing, also known as skeleton, is a variation of bobsleighing that involves athletes racing headfirst down a narrow, twisting ice track on a small sled. Unlike traditional bobsleighing, skeleton is an individual sport in which an athlete steers the sled as they navigate the course. Skeleton requires a high level of skill, speed, and courage, as athletes reach speeds of up to 87 miles per hour (140 kph) on the fastest tracks.

Skeleton athletes lie flat on their stomachs, with their heads down, and their faces just inches from the ice!

MADE TO GO FAST

A bobsleigh is typically made of a combination of materials such as steel, aluminum, and **fiberglass**. The frame is usually constructed from steel or aluminum to provide strength. The body of the bobsleigh is often made from fiberglass. This is lightweight and strong, and can be molded into **aerodynamic** shapes to reduce **drag**.

MODERN TOUCHES

Modern bobsleighs may also include other materials such as carbon fiber, which can give extra strength while keeping the overall weight of the sled as light as possible.

MAX SPEED, MAX CONTROL

The parts of a bobsleigh that come into contact with the ice are called runners. They are usually made of steel or other hard metals, and are carefully designed and shaped to provide maximum speed and control on the ice.

EXTREME NEED TO KNOW

Like traditional bobsleighing, skeleton is a dangerous sport that requires hours of training, experience, and safety equipment. Helmets, padding, and other protective gear must be worn, and athletes go through tough training to prepare for the physical demands of the sport.

Bobsleighs can reach speeds of up to 93 miles per hour (150 kph) on the fastest tracks.

ELANA SAYS NO MATTER WHERE YOU COME FROM, YOU CAN DO WINTER SPORTS, AND SHE HOPES TO INSPIRE OTHER GIRLS TO TAKE UP BOBSLEDDING.

Elana in action!

President Joe Biden greets Elana following her success at the 2022 Winter Olympic Games in Beijing.

ICE QUEEN

Elana Meyers Taylor is an American bobsledder who has become one of the most successful athletes in the history of the sport. Born on October 10, 1984, in Oceanside, California, Elana grew up playing a variety of sports before discovering bobsledding in college.

SLED STAR

Elana hit the bobsleigh track in 2007, and quickly became a rising star in the sport. She won her first World Championship medal in 2009, taking bronze in the mixed team event, and followed that up with a bronze at the 2010 Olympics in the same event.

OLYMPIC HAUL

Elana went on to win a medal in every Olympic Games that followed. In 2014 in Sochi, Russia, she narrowly missed out on gold by just 0.07 seconds! She added another silver in Pyeongchang in 2018, and a silver and bronze in Beijing, China, in 2022.

MEDALS AND RECORDS

As well as her Olympic success, the skilled bobsleigh star has also won many World Championship medals, including four golds, two silvers, and two bronzes. She has set a ton of track records and is known for her speed, power, and skill as a driver. Her achievements have made her a role model for young athletes around the world.

SPEED, SKATES, AND ICE

Ice cross, also known as ice cross downhill, is an extreme winter sport in which skaters race down a steep course on ice skates. The track features jumps, bumps, and obstacles that challenge even the most experienced skaters. Skaters need a high level of skill and nerves of steel to navigate the track.

PUSH AND SHOVE

Ice cross blends downhill skiing, hockey, and roller derby. It is often compared to sports such as **motocross** or BMX racing because it is so adrenaline-fueled. The race is a very quick, full-contact sport, with athletes pushing and shoving each other for the best position as they speed down the course.

FAST AND SMART

The goal is to reach the finish line in the shortest amount of time, while getting through the course and overtaking opponents. Skaters need speed, great skill, and the ability to make quick and smart decisions as they shoot across the ice.

"ICE CROSS SKATING—TO DO IT, YOU NEED TO BE FEARLESS."

Ice cross skaters love the combination of speed and skill.

Collisions are frequent in ice cross, so protective gear is a must.

EXTREME HISTORY

Ice cross began in Sweden in the early 2000s, and soon many people were taking on this super-fast, exciting new winter sport. The first ice cross event took place in 2001 in Stockholm, Sweden. The race was incredibly popular with both skaters and spectators, and soon, similar races began popping up all around Europe.

EASY ACCESS

The course for an ice cross event typically features steep drops, jumps, and sharp turns, and is often built in an **urban** setting. Unlike many other extreme winter sports, which take place in remote places, ice cross tracks are easy for competitors and **spectators** to get to. That draws in the crowds and makes for an amazingly exciting atmosphere at races.

HIGH-SPEED HIT

Many people, from spectators to skaters, love the sport for its high-speed thrills, with skaters pushing to be the fastest down the course. Athletes wear specialized protective gear, including helmets, kneepads, and other padding to protect against falls and collisions. The skates used in ice cross also have extra ankle support to provide better **stability** and control on the ice.

The blades on ice cross skates are razor-sharp to provide maximum grip.

SUPER SKATES

Ice cross skates have a low-cut boot, which helps skaters move more **flexibly** on a course. The boot is also heavily padded to protect against **impact** with the ice and other skaters. The blade of the skate is shorter and wider than a regular hockey blade, and is designed to help skaters cross the ice at speed, while keeping stable.

SHARP AND SAFE

In addition to being very sharp, ice cross skates also have **shock-absorbing** systems that can help reduce impact on the skater's joints, and special laces so the boots fit the riders comfortably and securely.

Skilled ice cross skaters take corners at spectacular speeds.

RACING FOR FAME

Competitive ice cross skating usually takes place on a closed track. Four skaters race against each other in **heats**, with the fastest skaters making it to the next round. From 2001 to 2018, races were part of the Red Bull Crashed Ice series, a worldwide championship in which top ice cross skaters competed for fame and prize money.

BIGGER AND BETTER

Since its early days, ice cross has continued to grow in popularity, with new events and courses being held around the world. In 2010, ice cross became part of the Winter X Games. Since 2019, the sport has been run by ATSX (All Terrain Skate Cross), which is the international governing body of ice cross. There are hopes that this action-packed sport will soon be part of the Winter Olympics.

EXTREME
NEED TO KNOW

Extreme ice cross skating can be dangerous because skaters reach speeds of up to 50 miles per hour (80 kph) and are at risk of falling or colliding with other skaters or obstacles on the track.

Today, ice cross is an amazingly popular extreme winter sport, with events held in countries around the world.

DOGS, SLEDS, AND SNOW RACES

Dog sledding, which is also known as mushing, is an extreme winter sport in which both people and dogs compete. Dog sledding began in the Arctic, as a means of getting across ice and snow. People traveled on a sled pulled by a team of trained dogs. Over time, dog sledding developed into a high-speed sport.

FOLLOW THE LEADER

A dog sled is designed to be lightweight and **maneuverable**, with runners that allow it to glide smoothly over snow and ice. The dogs are usually harnessed to the sled in pairs or teams. Lead dogs at the front of the team set the **pace** and direction, and the "wheel dogs" at the back provide extra power and stability.

A sled can be used to transport people, supplies, or equipment across snow-covered terrain.

In dog sledding, a sled is pulled by a team of dogs that are trained to work together. Each dog plays a specific role.

FOR FUN AND FOR SPORT

Dog sledding is popular for fun and as a competitive sport. In competitive dog sledding, teams race against each other over long distances—races range from short sprints to multi-day events covering many hundreds of snow-covered miles.

EXTREME NEED TO KNOW

Several breeds of dog are used in dog sledding, each with their own strengths and abilities that make them well-suited to the sport. Some of the most commonly used dog breeds include:

Alaskan Malamute: This strong and muscular dog is known for its ability to pull heavy loads over long distances.

Siberian Husky: This is a medium-sized breed, known for its speed and ability to work well in teams.

Samoyed: A friendly and intelligent dog, it has a thick coat of fur and is known for working well in cold weather.

Greenland Dog: This large, strong dog works well in the toughest and coldest conditions.

Canadian Eskimo Dog: This is a rare and ancient breed of dog that is known for its strength, loyalty, and ability to navigate difficult terrain.

Eurohound: This mixed-breed is a cross between a racing husky and a hunting dog. It is known for its speed and **endurance**.

THE WORLD'S WILDEST RACES

The biggest dog sled races in the world are usually held in the Arctic, where dog sledding has a long history. For fans of the sport, these are some of the best competitions in the world.

Finnmarksløpet

Where: Norway

The draw: people travel from all over the world to take part in this 621-mile (1,000 km) race through beautiful Norwegian countryside

Yukon Quest

Where: Canada

The draw: a 450-mile (724 km) race to Dawson City, passing through some of the most remote and beautiful landscapes in North America

Aviemore Sled Dog Rally

Where: Scotland

The draw: the largest race in the United Kingdom (UK), attracting competitors from across Europe

The Iditarod

Where: Alaska

The draw: covers 1,100 miles (1,770 km) of rugged terrain from Anchorage to Nome. It is probably the most challenging dog sled race in the world

La Grande Odyssée Savoie

Where: Mont Blanc, Europe

The draw: covers 560 miles (901 km), with very steep climbs and **descents** through the mountains

CHAPTER 3

BIKE IT, BOAT IT!

"SNOW AND BIKES, WHAT'S NOT TO LIKE?!"

Think you can't bike or boat across snow? It turns out you can! Extreme sportspeople have made it possible, and have taken their love of biking and boating to another level—onto the snow and ice.

Today, snow biking has become a popular winter sport around the world, with many ski resorts offering trails for snow bikes.

CYCLING IN THE SNOW

Snow biking, also known as snow mountain biking, is a winter sport in which people ride bikes with special tires that can take on snow-covered terrain. The tires on a snow bike are wider than traditional mountain bike tires, and have a tread that can grip the ground even when covered with snow and ice.

TURN, SLIDE, JUMP

People snow bike on trails, backcountry terrain, or even on ski slopes. Riders have a whole range of techniques to help them navigate the terrain, including **carving turns**, sliding, and jumping. Some snow bikers use a ski or snowboard to help control their speed and direction.

EXTREME HISTORY

Snow biking began in the early twentieth century, when bikes were used to get across snowy places. Later people added skis to the front wheels of their bikes, and rode them across the snow. This early version of snow biking was called "ski-biking."

BETTER BIKES, BETTER BIKING

Snow biking is becoming more and more popular, and the bikes are getting even more extreme as the sport develops. Bikes now have specialized fat tires, protective gear, and high-performance **suspension** systems to cope with the extreme terrain they travel across.

PUSHING TO THE LIMITS

As snow biking grows, so too do the sport's events and competitions. They are now held around the world. Riders compete to race downhill, freestyle jump, and backcountry explore. They constantly push the **boundaries** of what is possible on the snow.

NO BOUNDARIES

One of the first organized events that focused on extreme snow biking was the Red Bull Snow Boundaries race, which was held in Minnesota in 2016. It featured a challenging course that included jumps, steep hills, and tight turns. Top snow bike riders from around the world competed.

Snow scootering is another fun way to travel on snow.

Snowmobiles have made exploring the freezing wilderness easier—and more fun—than ever.

EXTREME AND HIGH-TECH

Technology has allowed people to get across the snow by bike faster than ever before—with snowmobiles. These are **motorized** bikes that have tracks to help them move over even deep snow. They have skis on the front for steering. And, best of all, they are really fun!

WILD ADVENTURES

Extreme snowmobilers take their machines on trails, backcountry terrain, and even on frozen lakes. The amazing vehicles allow them to adventure into the wild, and compete in races, freestyle events, and other competitions.

EXTREME NEED TO KNOW

Snowmobiling is fast, fierce, and fun, but, like all extreme sports, it requires a certain level of both skill and experience. Riders wear safety gear such as helmets, goggles, and protective clothing, and must be aware of the risks involved in the sport. It is also important that people respect the **environment** and stick to the trails wherever they travel.

TO THE EDGE

Snowmobilers push the limits of the sport with amazing maneuvers on difficult terrain. They ride on steep slopes, deep powder, and other challenging snow-covered places. Riders often have high-performance snowmobiles, which have more powerful engines and advanced suspension systems that allow them to navigate this tough terrain.

TOP OF HIS GAME

Brett Turcotte is a Canadian freestyle snowmobile rider who has become one of the top competitors in the sport. He was born on January 29, 1988 in British Columbia, Canada, and grew up riding snowmobiles.

MAKING A NAME

Brett began competing in freestyle snowmobiling events in his early 20s, and quickly made a name for himself with his impressive skills and maneuvers. He has won many Winter X Games gold medals, including in the Freestyle and Speed & Style events, and has also competed in the Snowcross World Championships.

NEW TRICKS, BIG STYLE

As well as being a competitive rider, Brett is known for his **innovative** tricks and incredible riding style. He always pushes the limits of what is possible on a snowmobile and has come up with amazing new moves, including the "Brett Turcotte backflip" and the "Kiss of Death." Brett is one of the greatest freestyle snowmobile riders of all time.

TRICKS, FLIPS, AND SPINS

Extreme snowmobiling maneuvers include jumping over obstacles, riding down steep and narrow chutes, and performing tricks such as flips or spins in the air. Riders need to be very fit and highly skilled to perform these stunts.

Snowmobile stunts are not for beginners to the sport!

KAYAKING ON SNOW

You've probably seen kayaking on the water, but you may not have seen it on the snow. Snow kayaking is an extreme sport in which kayakers shoot down snow-covered slopes, usually on a mountain or hill.

ULTIMATE CHALLENGE

Extreme snow kayaking is an adrenaline-fueled sport that takes snow kayaking to the next level. Extreme snow kayakers ride down steep and **treacherous** mountain slopes, through narrow chutes, over jumps, and off cliffs. They reach nail-biting speeds and perform stunts along the way.

EXTREME HISTORY

Snow kayaking probably began in the early 2000s, by people who loved kayaking on water and wanted to try it on snow. Those who enjoyed the thrill of riding **rapids** in the summer began to experiment with riding their kayaks down snowy slopes in the winter, **adapting** their techniques to the different terrain. The sport quickly became popular with adventurous kayakers and other extreme sports fans.

Snow kayakers often ride down specially designed courses or at terrain parks, which may include jumps, ramps, or other obstacles.

To kayak down a hill, first you have to get to the top!

BUILT FOR SNOW

Snow kayaks are specially designed. They are shorter and wider than traditional kayaks, and they have **reinforced hulls** and extra padding. They are made of super-tough plastic or other materials that can take the impact of hitting snow or ice. They also have specially designed runners or skis on the bottom to make them more stable and easier to control.

EXTREME PROTECTION

Safety and protection is vitally important for snow kayakers, so these extreme sportspeople wear protective gear, including helmets, goggles, and padded clothing.

NEW TO THE GAME

Snow kayaking is a new sport, and is not as widespread as other winter sports such as skiing or snowboarding. Since it is a niche sport, or a sport that is not widely practiced, there are only a few places in the world where people can experience snow kayaking. But where people can snow kayak, it can be an amazingly fun and special way to get around the snowy landscape.

"FREEDOM AND ADVENTURE—THAT'S SNOW KAYAKING."

THE WORLD'S SNOWIEST KAYAKING

For people who are brave enough to take on snow kayaking, there are some places in the world that test their skills to the extreme.

The Alps

Where: France

The draw: steep and difficult slopes that challenge even the most experienced kayaker

Hokkaido

Where: Japan

The draw: some of the deepest and driest snow in the world make it a snow kayaker's dream

Alaska

Where: United States

The draw: the ultimate in snow kayaking—deep snow and a wild landscape make snow kayaking here an incredible experience

Whistler

Where: Canada

The draw: amazing snow, amazingly steep slopes, and amazing views make Whistler a snow kayaking hotspot

Southern Alps

Where: New Zealand

The draw: a lot of different slopes that range in difficulty so there is something for everyone

CHAPTER 4

CLIMB IT, DIVE IT!

Ice can be difficult, dangerous, and deadly to cross. Its slippery surface is hazardous, and can cover the hidden dangers that lie beneath. But for some people, ice-covered landscapes offer a world of **exhilarating** sporting adventures. For them, ice-zones are playgrounds that can be climbed, skated, and even dived.

CONQUER THE ICE

When it comes to heading upward, ice climbing is probably one of the toughest ways to do it! Climbers use specialized equipment to **scale** ice formations, such as frozen waterfalls, **icefalls**, or glaciers. **Crampons**, ice axes, and other gear are used to grip the ice and climb upward.

TAKING A RISK

Ice climbing is difficult and challenging because of the unpredictable nature of the ice formations, as well as the harsh weather conditions in which climbs take place. Ice climbing requires a high level of skill, strength, and endurance.

Skilled ice climbers even navigate deep crevasses. →

ICE-CLIMBING WORLD

Ice climbing can be done outdoors and indoors. Outdoors, people head to alpine environments and glaciers. Some of the most popular places for ice climbing include the Canadian Rockies, the Alps, and the Himalayas. Indoor ice climbing centers are also great places to practice the sport.

BIGGER AND TOUGHER

Ice climbing became more and more popular through the twentieth century, as better equipment helped climbers scale bigger and tougher ice formations. In the 1970s and 1980s, ice climbing became a recognized sport, and many more people began to head to the ice.

NO LIMITS

Today, high-tech equipment has made it easier and safer for climbers to explore new and more difficult routes. Ice climbing is now popular around the world, with climbers tackling a lot of different ice formations and pushing what is possible to the limit.

EXTREME HISTORY

Ice climbing for sport or fun began in the middle of the nineteenth century in Europe. Switzerland and Norway were the go-to places for early adventurers. One of the earliest known ice climbs is believed to have taken place in the 1880s, when an English climber named William Cecil Slingsby made his way up one of the frozen waterfalls of the Geirangerfjord in Norway.

"ICE CLIMBING PUSHES YOU TO YOUR PHYSICAL AND MENTAL LIMIT."

Frozen waterfalls are a favored playground for adrenaline-seeking ice climbers.

Ice diving requires a high level of skill and experience.

DIVE IN!

Below the ice is a magical world, and it's one that draws in some of the most extreme sportspeople on Earth. They are ice divers. Ice diving is a type of scuba diving under the ice in a frozen area of water, such as a lake or river.

UNDER THE ICE

Ice diving takes place in bodies of water where the surface is covered by a layer of ice, often several feet thick. Divers cut a hole in the ice and enter the water, where they explore the area beneath.

EXTREME NEED TO KNOW

Ice diving is often done for research or exploration, as well as for sport. Ice divers use special equipment, such as diving suits and dive lights that are designed for cold water. Divers must be trained to dive safely and they learn how to navigate in **zero visibility** conditions, how to avoid becoming caught in ropes, and how to manage their air supply.

Jill is very aware of the risks and has developed techniques and equipment to help her keep safe.

ICE WORLD EXPLORER

Jill Heinerth is a Canadian underwater explorer, photographer, and filmmaker who has spent her life diving in some of the most extreme underwater environments on the planet. Her experience in ice diving and underwater exploration has made Jill one of the best ice divers in the world, and she is constantly pushing the boundaries of what is possible.

A LOVE OF DIVING

Jill was born on January 15, 1965 in Mississauga, Canada. As a child, she discovered that she loved the ocean and diving, and as she grew, so did her passion for the sport. The Canadian diver has plunged deep beneath the ice into extreme cold-water environments, completing many ice diving expeditions in places such as Antarctica and the Arctic. There, she has ventured into underwater ice caves and other extreme environments.

KEEPING SAFE

Ice diving is very dangerous. Its many hazards include extreme cold and poor visibility underwater—it is easy to become **disoriented** under the ice, and panic can quickly set in.

PASSIONATE PROTECTOR

Jill is also passionate about protecting the environment. She is involved in many research projects about climate change and its effects on the **polar regions**. She has worked with scientists to collect **data** and **samples** from beneath the polar ice to determine the effects of climate change.

JILL DESCRIBES ICE DIVING AS EXPLORING ANOTHER WORLD, WITH A STILLNESS THAT CAN'T BE FOUND IN ANY OTHER TYPE OF DIVING.

Ice diving is an incredibly exciting way to explore the underwater world.

THE WORLD'S COOLEST ICE DIVES

In all cases, divers only venture into the extreme cold water with a team of people to help keep them safe. For highly trained divers, here are some of the best places in the world to dive.

Finland

Where: Europe

The draw: there are lots of places to enjoy ice diving in Finland, which has some of the clearest and cleanest cold water in the world

Great Lakes

Where: United States and Canada

The draw: reliable winters make the Great Lakes an ice diver's paradise with many sites that are suitable for beginners

Norway

Where: Europe

The draw: many stunning dive sites in beautiful landscapes

Lake Baikal

Where: Russia

The draw: amazing cold-water diving in the deepest lake in the world

Antarctica

Where: Southern Ocean

The draw: clear waters and an incredible underwater landscape—a diver's dream

EXTREME GLOSSARY

adapting changing to better deal with something

adrenaline a hormone, or chemical messenger in the body, that creates a sense of excitement and a surge of energy

aerodynamic smoothly shaped to travel easily through air or water

athletes people who take part in sports, often competing at a high level

avalanche a violent movement of snow, ice, and rock down a slope

avalanche beacons small devices that transmit, or send, signals so that a person can be found if buried under snow during an avalanche

backcountry remote areas that are not regularly visited

boundaries the edges of something

bowls slopes and basins

carving turns a technique with which skis or snowboards are tilted on their edge to create smooth and controlled turns on the snow

chutes steep and narrow channels

climate change the gradual change in weather patterns and temperature over a long period of time

crampons metal devices with spikes worn on footwear to help climb snowy and icy areas

data information

descents downward journeys, usually on mountains

directed shown what to do

disoriented in a state of confusion and without a clear sense of direction

documentaries nonfiction films

drag the force of resistance created when an object moves through air or water

elite the best at something

endurance doing something, such as a physical activity, for a long time

environment the natural surroundings

exhilarating very exciting

extreme sportspeople people who do high-risk sports

fiberglass a reinforced plastic material

flexibly bending easily

gender equality the idea of equality between males and females

glaciated refers to landscapes that have been shaped by glaciers

glaciers large bodies of ice

gravity the force that pulls objects toward other large objects

halfpipes U-shaped structures used to perform maneuvers

heats rounds of a sporting competition

hulls the frame of a ship or boat

icefalls sections of descending ice

impact when one object comes forcibly into contact with another object

innovative describes a smart new idea or way of doing something

maneuverable easy to move

maneuvers moves skilfully or carefully

motocross a form of off-road motorcycle racing held on enclosed off-road circuits

motorized fitted with a motor

navigate to travel using a series of actions or a specified course

off-piste describes traveling away from a usual route

pace the rate of how quickly or slowly something happens

polar regions areas near the North and South Poles

powder freshly fallen snow that is light and fluffy

probes instruments used to find or investigate things

professional describes a person who does a sport or another activity as a way of earning money

propel to push forward

rapids fast-moving areas of water in a river or stream

reinforced made stronger

remote far away from other people or things

samples small sections of something

scale the act of climbing a vertical or steep surface

Scandinavian relates to countries in Northern Europe that include Denmark, Norway, Sweden, and Finland

shock-absorbing describes something that is able to absorb the energy of an impact

skeleton a winter sport in which a person rides a small sled, known as a skeleton bobsled, down a frozen track while lying face down and head-first

sleds land vehicles that slide across a surface, usually of ice or snow. They are also called skids, sledges, or sleighs

snow parks outdoor complexes that contain terrain and human-made features for skiers and snowboarders to perform tricks. They are also called terrain parks

spectators people who watch an event or sport

stability being stable or steady

stunts unusual or difficult tricks that skilled people perform

suspension the system of springs and shock absorbers by which a vehicle is supported on its wheels

terrain the physical characteristics of a particular area of land. Terrain can range from flat and open to rugged and mountainous

terrain parks outdoor complexes that contain terrain and human-made features for skiers and snowboarders to perform tricks. They are also called snow parks

trails marked paths or routes often used for skiing, hiking, biking, or other outdoor activities

treacherous describes something that is full of danger

tree wells very dangerous and deep areas that form in snow around the base of trees

urban describes cities, towns, or other areas with many buildings and people

venturing exploring something new

zero visibility unable to see anything

FIND OUT MORE

BOOKS

DISCOVER MORE ABOUT EXTREME SPORTS WITH THESE GREAT READS.

Allan, John. *Snowboarding* (Adventure Sports). Hungry Tomato, 2022.

Eason, Sarah. *Dig Deep! Extreme Land Sports* (Ultimate Sports). Cheriton Children's Books, 2024.

Eason, Sarah. *Don't Look Down! Extreme Air Sports* (Ultimate Sports). Cheriton Children's Books, 2024.

Eason, Sarah. *Take a Deep Breath! Extreme Water Sports* (Ultimate Sports). Cheriton Children's Books, 2024.

George, Enzo. *Physical Science in Snow and Ice Sports* (Science Gets Physical). Crabtree Publishing, 2020.

Spilsbury, Louise. *Snow and Ice Sports* (Sports for Supergirls). Gareth Stevens Publishing, 2019.

WEBSITES AND ORGANIZATIONS

THESE WEBSITES ARE GREAT FOR LEARNING MORE ABOUT THE WORLD OF SNOW AND ICE SPORTS, AND IF YOU WANT TO TRY YOUR HAND AT SOME SPORTS, YOU CAN START YOUR JOURNEY HERE.

Learn more about winter sports at:
https://kids.britannica.com/students/article/winter-sports/277771

Discover facts about snow and ice sports at the Winter Olympics:
www.natgeokids.com/uk/discover/history/general-history/winter-olympics-facts

Learn more about snowboarding and freeskiing at the United States of America Snowboard and Freeski Association (USASA):
https://www.usasa.org

Find out more about snowboarding and watch some amazing videos at:
www.boardriding.com/associations/united-states-of-america-snowboard-and-freeski-association-usasa

Publisher's note to educators and parents:
All the websites featured above have been carefully reviewed to ensure that they are suitable for students. However, many websites change often, and we cannot guarantee that a site's future contents will continue to meet our high standards of educational value. Please be advised that students should be closely monitored whenever they access the Internet.

INDEX

ABOUT THE AUTHOR

Sarah Eason is an experienced children's book author who has written many books about sport and sport science. She would love to visit some of the amazing places researched while writing this book, and (maybe!) try out some extreme sports there.